Content-

Feeling Loved

On the bay of your memories
I'm waiting for your steps to fall
In the sky of our similarities
I'm waiting for your voice to call
In the space of our closeness
I'm waiting for you to touch my soul
On the land of our differences
I'm waiting for you to meet my soul
Protecting you has become my role
Falling for you from my every mole
Together we can be our console
Not separating like the two dipole
My heart that you have stole
Not apart now we are one whole
When I see you, excitement I can't control
I'll catch you at your downfall
I'll protect you like a firewall
Together we become whole...

When you'll be alone, I'll stay
When you are broken, I'll pray
I'll make you happy every night and day
You run through me like my blood sway
I'll give you comfort when you lay
I lost myself when you say hey
Without you I can't imagine my life a single day
To reach to you soon, I'm gonna find my way...

Whether i could be with you or not
There's not a probability
Still there's a possibility
That I'll respect your dignity

Even if I don't care about you
You're still my responsibility
When you're around, i fly
Like there's no gravity

When i see your smile
My heart generates electricity
Even if I'm not with you
You're my spirit and my spirituality

You try to stay away
But there's no resistivity
There is so much complexity
That i started doubting my capability

I'm surrounded with insecurity
I'm full of negativity
I can't hate you more than this
Because you're still my priority...

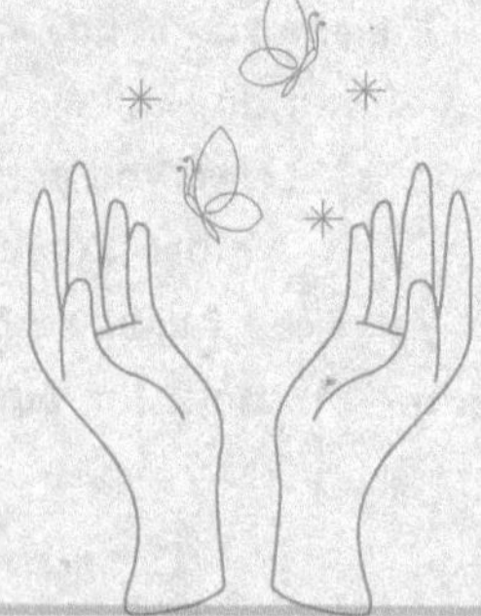

I'll carry your burden
I'll cherish your life
I'm here only for you, cuz
You're my whole life

I adore you with my heart
You're that beautiful girl
Your heart is like an ocean
Your heartbeat is like a pearl...

I didn't raise you
But I'll praise you
Wherever you will go
I'm gonna chase you

Don't be scared of the world
I know your will
You're my strength
And you're my skill...

You're my first ray in the morning
You're my sunshine of the noon
You're my sunset in the evening
And you're my moonlight in the night
You're the fragrance of the first rain on the soil
You're the rainbow of my happiness
You're my coldness in the summer
You're my warmness in the winter
You're my love, you're now my peace...

I put my faith in and I'll stay
Grab my hand and I'll pray
Defeating the darkness
And I'll rise again and today
I promise that i won't be late
I promise, it won't be delay
Hey god listen to my pray
And I'm gonna find my way
An important part that I'll play
I'll reshape my life like it's some clay
Trust in me and I won't betray
Today or tomorrow I'll find my way...

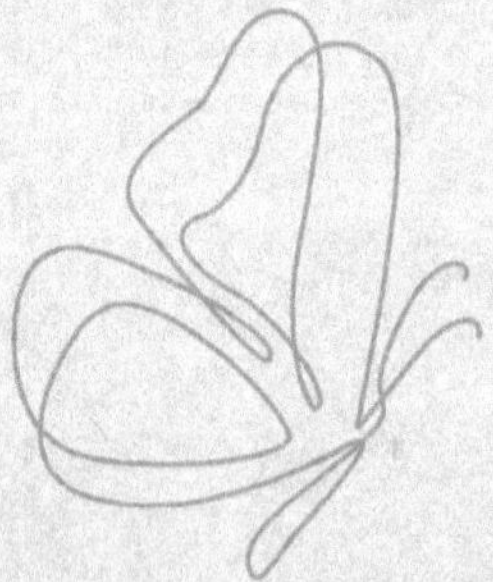

My heart feels warmth
With the warmth of your gaze
When i look into your eyes
I feel like I'm lost in a maze
If you tried to go away
I'll follow your every trace
I'll go beyond on my chase
Every moment with you,
That I will praise
My face will shine like a star
If you're with me in my good
And in my every bad phase...

I want to be an open book to you
Nothing should be hidden
Nothing should be forbidden
Every reason for the tear
Now has to be forgiven
It was neither your mistake
It was neither my mistake
Destiny has just played with us
And now our hearts are at stake
Whatever I was, I'm much better now
Whatever happened to us
I just want to forget all the reasons now
Again I'm at the turn
From where i started my journey
Still waiting for that 'yes'
That i always wanted to hear
Today again, i want you by my side to cheer...

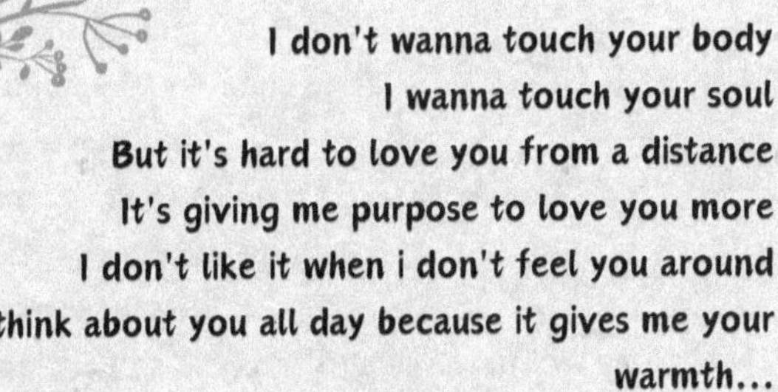

I don't wanna touch your body
I wanna touch your soul
But it's hard to love you from a distance
It's giving me purpose to love you more
I don't like it when i don't feel you around
I think about you all day because it gives me your
warmth...

I waited for you,
Like a cuckoo waits for monsoon
I looked out of the gazing window
And felt like your steps fell into my place
My heart is falling for you,
Just like a feather falls from sky
My heart is feeling numb and my hands are shaking
When we contact each other through the eyes,
I bloody hell no idea, why the hell I'm sweating
Everyday I look at you
And you pass like a stranger
How am I supposed to win your heart
My poems needs to be my messenger
Still I'm hoping, someday you will talk to me
Still I'm waiting, someday you will walk to me
If you will be in my destiny,
Every time, the world will bring you back to me...

Smile that is precious to me
Laugh that i always miss
You shouldn't be so much worried
As I'm always beside you
I know there's so much love for me inside you
Whenever you feel alone,
Whenever you feel scared
You will find a beautiful place somewhere beside you
It's my heart where I'll permanently reside you...

Broken Heart

In the cold desert of my life
You were like some sand
That i tried to hold
Through my bare naked hand
You're like a wave now
Who is hurting it's shore
Still I'm looking for some reason
To love you more and more
Cold memories now makes me laugh
Bitter truths now gives me satisfaction
I'm facing the devil inside me and
I just want to be out of this affection...

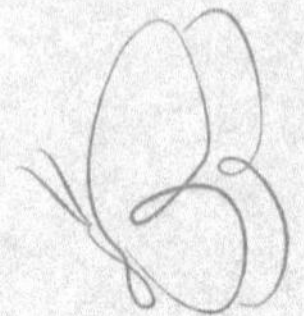

The roads seem very empty now
Feels like I'm lost in some mist
The rain drops tries to fade away the mist
So that I can see my path on my own
But the thunder still wrenches my heart
It trembles the earth beneath my foot
I'm scared when I hear my own footsteps
Hallucinating someone is following me
But it's none other than my own shadow
That I'm afraid of...

There's never been a day
I haven't thought of you
There's never been a moment
I haven't waited for you
My inspiration is gone
My heart chooses to be alone
My eyes still wait for you
As they've seen how everything went wrong
I just take a deep breath
And i just close my eyes
But as i think about moving on
All I see is your face on and on
Look how destiny has won...

Not knowing what the hell is wrong
A very dissonant, life has played a song
I'll be honest, i didn't hit a bong
But somehow this journey seems very long
On the pages I was writing my story
I thought i could make it my glory
It's a huge burden to carry
What I thought is practical
All was just a nonsense theory
It's just a game between life and death
I thought I'll show you my wrath
Somehow i manage to speak
But sometimes it's harder to breath...

I don't love anymore
I don't care anymore
Feelings that were hidden
I don't hide anymore
Was lost in a sea but now I've reached the shore
Suffered alone but can't take it anymore
Wanna escape but can't find any door
I put myself in the dark
Where you can't look for
I'm just going really far
Now you can't hurt me anymore...

Happiness that was lost
Feelings that were hidden in a box
Came out somehow from somewhere
Now I'm seeing my lost happiness
Once again and everywhere
I don't want to grab your hand again
But everything still feels the same
My hopes weren't wrong and I see
Once again you called my name
I thought my truths were my lie
But you were the star of my eye
I don't wanna ask, how-when and why
Now we don't look at each other and get high...

Messed up with my own life
Curses are falling under my skies
Troubled with my true lies
And my ghosts are becoming my spies
Darkness surrounds me from everywhere
Trenches are forward that I'm unaware
Wishing my thoughts to disappear
The pain belongs to me which is not to share
All i learnt is that, nobody care
Putting forward my life for God to spare
Wishing i had somebody behind me to cheer
But when I looked back i found that nobody care...

My smile starts fading away
My fondness starts getting away
My truths are becoming a lie
My lips are murmuring like a fly
My mind is bursting and nobody cares
I'm burning myself with my own flares...

I know my efforts can go effortless
I know I won't be able to make a change
The place I'm trying to take in your heart
The efforts I'm showing to be your part
It's all happening like a tragedy
My way is all out of my destiny
Truth lies behind my simplicity
My silence is now on my priority...

Something feels like i lost it
I wish things could have been different
My sorrow is not letting me move on
But I'm helpless in my own war
I don't know what I'm insecure about
I don't know why i fucking care
But this chapter will also pass
As much as I feel left out alone
My fear is that I'll stop caring
My fear is that I'll be alone in the end
But I believe it's not the end
Because I'll forge my own history
Trying to get better everyday
Trying to fight like a warrior
One day you are gonna lose me
And you won't even realise it
Someday I'm gonna turn my back on you
You will regret the moments of your life
But there will be nothing you can do
Because you have already lost me forever...

I'll get back but maybe I've fallen
I'll heal back but maybe I'm broken
I'm standing still but maybe I'm frozen
I try to remember but maybe I'm forgotten
It's not my destiny but maybe I'm chosen
I want to achieve it but maybe I'm forbidden
I'm living in truth with the lies I've spoken
I try to remember but maybe I'm forgotten...

Feelings that are hard to explain
Thoughts that are enough to numb you
Confidence that is beneath the ground
Around the people, who want to chump you
Wanna get up but burdened by my own weight
Wanna cheer up but silent through my own fate
Wanna run away but closed by my own gate
Wanna follow my guts but my heart is my own threat
Facing the demons, that are living in my head
I'm a clown of the game that destiny has played
Nobody's gonna listen to the prayers I've prayed
Couldn't go so far hence my hopes have been dead...

Smiles that were auspicious
Moments that were precious
Life is getting harder and,
Dreams are becoming vicious
The tougher & tougher I get
The weaker & weaker I become
Hiding my pain in my eyes
Drowning myself under my lies
Wanna be out, out of my sorrow
Hoping my pain will end tomorrow
I can forget you and your love
But can't forget your treacheries
Feeling I can hardly lose
But what about your memories...

I remember how we met
I remember how we fell
I felt like I'm independent
But i got caught in my own jail
I followed your trace
I've seen every face
I'm not gonna chase you now
I've got caught in a maze
It's all about destiny
It's all about my fate
Whatever decision I will make
Later I'm gonna just hate
You have become a trait
Dunno how along we get
I chose to be alone but
I still remember how we met...

The shadows are walking behind me
The nightmares are sitting beside me
The horror is making me frightened
The darkness is living inside me
The hopes have been crumbled
The thoughts have been shattered
Slowly-Slowly, I'm losing it all
Everyone & Everything that mattered...

Can you abrupt my mind
For the light moment
Can you feel my heart
Just to shine away
Can you see my laugh
Just to find a way
Can you please my eyes
For the past we had
Can you shock my nerves
For the life we have
Can you cheer me up
Just to rise again
Can you heal my soul
For the pain, you've given
Can you heal my heart
For the trust, you've broken...

Words are not enough to tell you my story
It's having a bad phase but it will be my glory
As I'm heading, I'm hating the words like sorry
As long as it's painful, it will be my story
I feel it and observe everything, yes I'm quite aware
You look at my face and tell me, does it look like i care ?
I trusted and shared everything that i don't really share
Wasted my feelings on you that were really-really rare
You taught me to fly like a beautiful feather
Now you just tear me apart like I'm a piece of paper...

Don't wanna cry and don't wanna shout
Desperately I've been thinking about
Somethings that I'm realising now
I can be alone and i don't have any doubt
Shaken but now I've awaken
Bonds, that can easily be broken
Words, that i never had spoken
Truth if i told, i don't beg any pardon
Lies have been running around me
Fear has been murmuring around me
Trust that has been torned
Life that is being mourn
Responsibilities that have been forced
Sometimes i wonder, why am I born...

Time flies and people change
The one who meant everything
Are now just becoming stranger
I was meant to be alone
But you grabbed my hand
Feels like you're losing it now
And I'm going as far away as possible
Ran behind you, fought beside you
Now running from my own wishes
Now fighting with my own choices...

Maybe it's time to say goodbye
Maybe I should stop for a moment and wait
The idea of sitting behind is just pushing me away
I really want to talk about it
But if I did, I'll lose a lot
My thoughts are not letting me sleep
My thoughts are not getting me peace
All I know is that it was wrong
But whatever this is, I'm not ready to talk
Because if I did, I'll lose a lot
I wanna share and I wanna care
But I don't want myself to get hurt
I want to put you first but now
I'm really afraid of leaving myself behind
I won't be able to trust you now
I won't be able to be someone who i used to be
So just leave me as I'm right now...

The vicious life is laughing at me
The unknown lies are mocking me
I've just become a clown to laugh
My silence is now taunting me
I will run away, wanna be alone
I'm becoming the villain of my own
Thoughts that were keeping me here and
Dreams I saw with you just needed to be thrown...

Wondering how the values are changing
Wondering how the relationships are ending
Words have no longer meaning and bonds are breaking
I'm still wondering how my place new people are taking
Without any drink why my hands are shaking
How much I put myself in your making
I put my heart in your well being
Still feeling like somewhere I'm lacking

I fall for the words
They are nothing but the broken promises
I fall for the efforts
They are nothing but an act
I fall for the honesty
It's nothing but a mask
I fall for the loyalty
It's nothing but a task
I tried my best
But i couldn't get so far
In the end, I know I'll loose
So it's nothing but a war
Turned myself, changed myself
Nothing got me the right
Someday you'll lose me
Because now it's a fight
I tried to boost myself
I know I tried a lot
But eventually it's falling apart
Everything you do now
Is just ripping off my heart...

Walking frightened & alone in the night
Moving my steps left to right
Cold started shivering me high
Everything is getting out of my sight
I know, i know this is my fight
But I can't see the hope of my light
Every time harder & harder, i tried
Watching myself, losing my pride
Everything started getting out of hand
Watching myself, going to the end...

I waited for you
In the hot sun and even in the rain
As I feel the water droplets
Falling over my cheeks
I come to realise it's not just been days
But I have been here for some weeks
I'm not the same anymore,
Who will fall into your rubbish tricks
I'm not a football anymore
That everyone just kicks
You should know me better
I relied upon my ghosts and my freaks
I come to understand
It comes with great risks, and here I tell you
I'm not falling for some damn beautiful chicks...

प्रेम गीत

बारिश की बूंदों की तू सरगम लागे रे,
ताप मे भी छाया सी तू सरमन लागे रे ।
सच्चे दिल की तू जैसे कोई दर्पण लागे रे,
अपने दिल की डोर से तू मेरे मन को सांचे रे ।
भागे भागे इन काली सड़के, अंधे मोड़ो पर,
तू साथ तो ना कोई अड़चन लागे रे ।
मन मेरा कोयला, तू जैसे कोई हीरा लागे रे,
बिन तेरे ही जग सुना, निर्मुला, कुछ फिका लागे रे ।
सुंदरता तेरी जो मेरे मन को भावे रे,
दूरियां तेरी जो मेरे मन को सतावे रे ।
स्मिता तेरी जो मेरे दिल को हसावे रे,
बारिश की बूंदों को तू सरगम लागे रे ।
बारिश की बूंदों को तू सरगम लागे रे ।।

तेरी बाते रिझाए मेरे मन को
तेरी हसी मुस्कुराए मेरे मन को
तेरे मुखड़े में चांद सा जो नूर है
तेरा साथ ही अब मेरा गुरूर है
सुखी रोटी भी तेरे संग मीठी लागे रे
परछाइयों में भी तेरे साथ की सुगंध आवे रे
कलियों को छूकर फूल बनादे
ऐसा तेरा खुमार रे
मुझ जैसे को भी अपना बनाले
ऐसा तेरा प्यार रे

गुलों में खिली कली की तरह कोमल है तू
मिट्टी में गिरी हुई बारिश की महक है तू
सुबह सुनाई देने वाली चिड़ियों की चहक है तू
मेरे दिल में धड़कने वाली धड़क है तू
मेरा जीवन जीवन नही, तेरा घर बन गया है
इस घर में तेरे कदमों से खुशी छा जाएगी
ये घर एक दम सुना हो जायेगा
जब जब तू इस घर को छोड़कर,एक कदम भी दूर जायेगी
मेरी खामोशी को खामोशी न समझ
ये तो बस तेरे लिए मेरा बहुत सारा प्यार है
मेरी पुरानी बातो को याद कर नाराज न हो,
इतना ही समझ की ये मेरा ऐतबार है

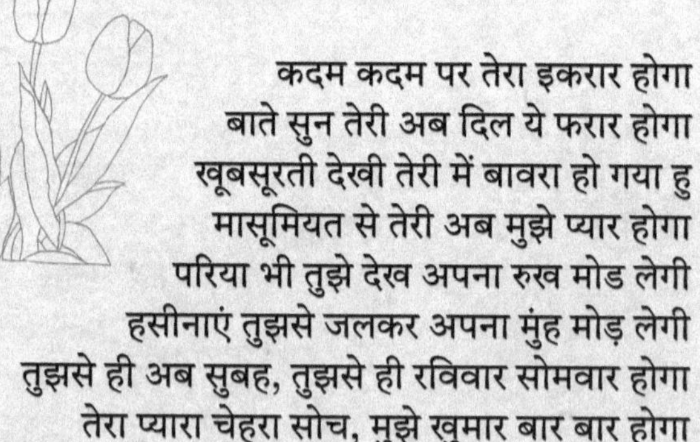

कदम कदम पर तेरा इकरार होगा
बाते सुन तेरी अब दिल ये फरार होगा
खूबसूरती देखी तेरी में बावरा हो गया हु
मासूमियत से तेरी अब मुझे प्यार होगा
परिया भी तुझे देख अपना रुख मोड लेगी
हसीनाएं तुझसे जलकर अपना मुंह मोड़ लेगी
तुझसे ही अब सुबह, तुझसे ही रविवार सोमवार होगा
तेरा प्यारा चेहरा सोच, मुझे खुमार बार बार होगा

तुझ बिन हर सांस अधूरी सी है
तू साथ तो हर दुआ अब पूरी सी है
लगता था मुझे की अब बस हम दूर हो गए
तेरी डांट भी मेरे लिए सुरीली सी है
वो लम्हा अब भी याद है जब तुझे पहली बार देखा था
मन में ख्याल आया तू वहा क्यों आ गई
लेकिन जैसे जैसे तुझे मैं सुनता गया
पता ही नहीं चला और मुझमें तू समा गई
गिरते हुए इस मंज़र को तेरा सहारा मिल गया
तुझे छू कर जैसे दिल आवारा बन गया

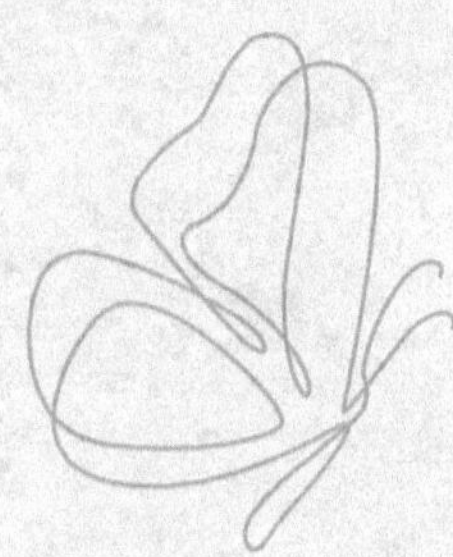

मेरी लगन फिर से तुझमें लगने लगी है
तेरा इंतजार फिर से अब सताने लगा है
जो आंखे तेरे इंतजार में सुख गई है
अब फिर से मेरा दिल तुझमें समाने लगा है
क्या जो मैं सोच रहा हु, वह सही है
या ये सब कुछ सिर्फ मेरा भ्रम है
बस फिर से तेरे हां कहने की ही देरी है

ताज महल के संगमरमर सी
सुरीले गीतों की सरगम सी
सुंदरता के उदाहरण जैसी
साफ दिल की तू दर्पण सी

शब्दजाल

अब कुछ ऐसे माहौल में ढल सा गया हु,
वक्त के साथ में काफी हद तक बदल सा गया हु।
जिस गुमनामी में, मैने तेरे सपने संजोए थे,
उन सपनों को खुद ही बिखेर कर, संभल सा गया हु।।
हवाओ में भी अब तेरी खुशबू की महक नही आती,
बंद आंखों से जो दिखाई देती है अब वो कही नजर नहीं आती।
जो दूर होकर भी जो पास थी,
जो अंधेरे में भी मेरी रोशनी की आस थी।
मैं कभी सोच ही नही पाया कि,
वो मेरे टूटते हुए सपनो का आगाज थी।।
सवेरा भी तेरा हुआ करता था,
शाम में भी तेरा ही इंतजार था।
सब कुछ भूल गया हु तेरे बारे में, बस,
यही नहीं भूल पाया कि तू मेरा प्यार था।।।

सपनो के जहान में आसमान चाहिए
तकदीर के दरवाजे का फरमान चाहिए
हुस्न के रंगों में हम भी कही मिल गए थे
रंगों को धो लू बस ऐसा इक अरमान चाहिए
टूटी हुई कश्ती पर भी निडर बन जाऊ
साथ निभाने वाला एक अनजान चाहिए
दूरियों को भी भुलाकर अपना बनाले
मुझ पर फक्र करने वाला एक इंसान चाहिए

अब कहना भी छोड़ दिया है
अब सहना भी छोड़ दिया है
वक्त ने कुछ ऐसी करवट ली है की
खुद के साथ अब वक्त बिताना भी छोड़ दिया है
बचकानी बातो पर अब
मुस्कुराना भी छोड़ दिया है
तेरी फिक्र करते करतें, अब
खुद से रुख भी मोड़ लिया है

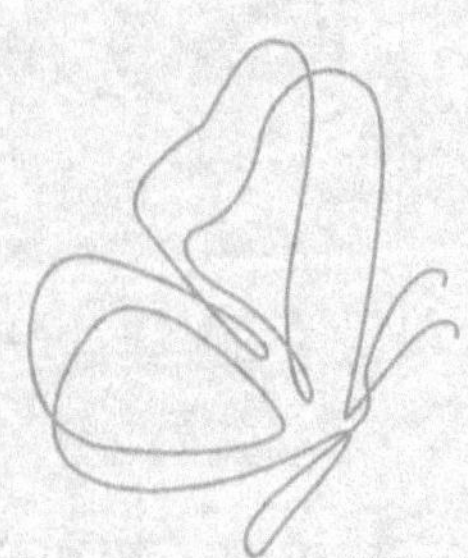

हर लम्हा कुछ टूटा-टूटा सा है
हर कतरा क्यों जुदा-जुदा सा है
परछाइयों ने भी साथ छोड़ दिया है
उम्मीद का दिया क्यों बुझा-बुझा सा है
दिल क्यों कुछ रूठा-रूठा सा है
हर सच भी अब झूठा-झूठा सा है
कुछ खास रंग नहीं अब जिंदगी में
फिर भी सब अनूठा-अनूठा सा

ख्यालों और सपनो में खोया जा रहा हूं,
ख्वाइशों के तले में डुबोया जा रहा हूं
राही बनकर रह गया हूं खुद की ही राह में
उलझनों के बादल में संजोया जा रहा हूं।

अंधेर नगरी में
एक उजाला मिल गया था
तेरे जैसा यार मानो
सितारा मिल गया था
खूबसूरती तेरी परियों से भी परे थी
खुशनसीब समझा खुद को
तुझसा यारा मिल गया था
आसमा भी तेरे आगे
झुक जाया करता था
जब भी तू अपनी
पलखे उठाया करता था
नदिया भी तेरे लिए
गीत गाया करती थी
हवा भी तुझे छूकर
तुझसे लिपट जाया करती थी
किस्मत वाला होगा जो भी तेरे
कदमों में पायल पहनाएगा
मैं कभी सोच ही नहीं सका कि
तू इक दिन किसी और का हो जायेगा

Manish R. Trivedi

manishtrivedi563@gmail.com